D0579857

Frontispiece. Altar of the Virgin of Guadalupe, church of Hoctun, Yucatan. The altar is decorated with paper roses similar to the ones the Virgin caused to grow in winter for Juan Diego. The hill of Tepeyac with churches dedicated to the Virgin of Guadalupe is painted on the wall behind the altar.

MEXICAN CELEBRATIONS

Eliot Porter and Ellen Auerbach

Essays by Donna Pierce and Marsha C. Bol

University of New Mexico Press, Albuquerque

LIBRARY OF CONGRESS CATALOGING-IN-PUBLICATION DATA

Porter, Eliot, 1901–
    Mexican celebrations / Eliot Porter and Ellen Auerbach ; essays by
Donna Pierce and Marsha Bol. — 1st ed.
      p. cm.
   ISBN 0–8263–1209–8
    1. Fasts and Feasts—Mexico.   2. Fasts and feasts—Catholic
Church.   3. Catholic Church—Mexico.   4. Mexico—Religious life and
customs.   I. Auerbach, Ellen, 1906–   .   II. Pierce, Donna.
III. Bol, Marsha.   IV. Title.
BX1428.2.P67   1990
263'.9'0972—dc20

                                                    90–12100
                                                    CIP

Contents

Foreword

In the fall of 1986, I was asked to write an essay for a book of photographs taken by Eliot Porter and Ellen Auerbach in Mexico in the 1950s, called *Mexican Churches*. I went to Porter's studio to begin viewing the photographs that had been selected. As Porter, curator Janet Russek, and I looked through the slides and 4 x 5 negatives, we soon realized that he and I had visited the same sites approximately thirty years apart—Porter in the 1950s, myself in the 1980s.

Eliot Porter first visited Mexico briefly in 1951 with his wife, Aline, and then later returned for an extensive photographic expedition accompanied by a New York photographer friend, Ellen Auerbach. Porter and Auerbach covered more than 11,000 miles from November 1955 to late April 1956. They took over 3,000 photographs, mostly in color, using two 35mm, two 2¼ reflex, and two 4 x 5 view cameras plus a 16mm movie camera.

For interior views, particularly in churches, they used 35mm color film with no artificial lighting, and Porter later made the dye-transfer prints. In an attempt to capture the special atmosphere within the churches, they relied exclusively on the existing light from high windows, open doors, candles, and a few stray light bulbs. As a result, they often worked in virtual darkness with tripods and very long exposures. Porter and Auerbach agreed at the time that using artificial illumination would have been like "photographing the dawn with flashbulbs."

Porter lent me his travel journal to help in the writing of the essay. In reading through the lists of photographs taken each day, I realized what a wealth of information the pictures offered on colonial art and architecture, religious rituals, pre-Columbian temples and ruins, markets, landscapes, and daily life in Mexico in the 1950s. Several years later, when the decision was made to publish a second book of the photographs, I was thrilled at the opportunity to look through all 3,000 photographs with Porter.

We began in July of 1988. As we discussed each photograph at length, I was impressed at the amount of detail he remembered after thirty years. Porter wanted to know the fate of the churches, saints, and traditions. We commiserated over places that have been "modernized" in the interim and rejoiced at sites that have been declared historic monuments and are now protected by the Mexican government. We discussed the rituals and celebrations and worried about their future.

After years of studying the colonial art and traditions of Mexico, I was delighted to see such extensive photodocumentation in color of the original location of many well-known objects as well as images that have since disappeared. I had recently been traveling in Mexico with a team from the Metropolitan Museum of Art of New York in preparation for an exhibition on Mexican art. We had seen a lovely section of an altar screen in a museum in Querétaro with paintings that were obviously from a later period than the screen. We wondered where it was from and about the nature of the original paintings. I found the answer in the Porter and Auerbach photographs. They had taken several views of the altar screen with its original paintings in its previous location in the church of Acolman.

I was also pleased to see the Porter and Auerbach photographs of the nave frescoes in the church at Huejotzingo. Painted in the sixteenth century, these images of Holy Week processions have been alternately covered over and rediscovered through the centuries. When I visited the church in 1978, they were not visible. Several years later a Baroque altar screen was moved and the paintings exposed from behind it. At that time they were restored, along with other paintings on the nave walls, as part of a government project. The paintings are important not only for their artistic value but also as documentation of a European tradition transplanted to the New World in the early colonial period. Since Huejotzingo is a functioning church, however, the altar screens have been replaced, once more covering over the restored paintings.

As part of the living tradition of Catholicism in Mexico, religious images are often moved around and placed in new locations as the seasons or times change. A well-known image of the Virgin of the Apocalypse from the sixteenth-century church of Xochimilco has been relocated several times through the years. While the figure was originally made as the central image of the upper section of the main altar screen, photographs taken during the 1940s show the Virgin in a recessed niche in the cloister of the convent attached to the church. When Porter and Auerbach photographed her, she had been placed in a high window in the nave of the church, silhouetted by the light from behind. Fortunately, she is back in her original location at the present time, presiding over the main altar screen.

Significant folk customs were documented by Porter and Auerbach, including some that have since become scarce or in danger of extinction. For example, their photographs of *Incendios* (Passion or Fire) altars dedicated to the Sorrows of the Virgin document an important Lenten tradition. The construction of these uniquely Mexican altars had almost died out by the early 1980s, although a revival is currently underway with the encouragement of museums and folklorists. Many religious celebrations in Mexico are recorded in the Porter and Auerbach photographs – either directly, in views of ritual participants, or indirectly, in images of ephemeral decorations or specially adorned saints.

During this project, it has become obvious that even after many photographic expeditions all over the world, the trip to Mexico remains a special memory to both Porter and Auerbach. Their affection for Mexico is clearly apparent in their photographs which not only document many Mexican customs and works of art, but also reflect a sensitive attempt to record the culture in its own light. In their time-consuming effort to produce honest images of life in Mexico, they managed to capture the atmosphere that envelops the people and places. The result is a photographic celebration of the people of Mexico and their living rituals.

Donna Pierce
Santa Fe, New Mexico

A Living Ritual

In Mexico religion punctuates everyday life. Roadsides are dotted with grotto shrines and flowered memorial crosses. Truck fenders sport day-glow religious decals and Virgins grace dashboards. Doors to homes are topped with straw or wooden crosses to prevent the entry of evil, and window sills frame statues of saints. Religious images, candles, and decorations line the shelves in urban department stores. In rural areas, white-painted rocks spell out the names of saints or form large crosses on hillsides. Burros loaded with flowers grown for specific religious festivals head toward regional markets.

Everyday life also permeates religion in Mexico. Walls of pilgrimage shrines are covered with paintings depicting moments in people's lives that required divine intervention. Churches are decorated for ceremonies marking the major events of human life – baptism, first communion, marriage, and death. Special religious festivals often correlate with planting and harvesting cycles. Farm animals are ceremonially blessed once a year. The integration of life and religion is reflected in the Christian rituals celebrated throughout the year.

Since the early Christian era, the retelling of the fundamental Christian stories through readings, art, architecture, theater, and music has been an important aspect of religious education. Because of persecution during the early period, people often told the stories of the life of Christ through allegories and symbols, such as Christ as the Good Shepherd or the Lamb of God. During the Middle Ages, accounts of the lives of the growing number of saints were added to the many legends of Christianity. Among a largely illiterate populace, everyone was able to decipher the teachings of the church in the sculptures, stained glass windows, passion plays, processions, and hymns.

In Mexico the concept of presenting the Christian stories mostly through the visual arts was enhanced by a similar tendency towards pageantry inherent in ancient Mexican traditions. The church, its decoration, and festivals functioned as a visual "Bible" that even the illiterate and people speaking different Indian dialects could "read." In Mexico today, worshippers can read the Christian narratives on the altar screens, the saints act out their own stories in processions, and church decorations indicate seasonal rituals to be celebrated.

Christianity was introduced to Mexican soil on Easter Sunday in 1519 when the chaplain with Hernando Cortés, the Spanish conqueror of Mexico, celebrated the first Mass on the continent of North America. Letters between Cortés and the King of Spain, Charles I, list the evangelization of the New World as a main priority of the conquest. When the conquest was completed in 1521, Cortés sent immediately for twelve Franciscans to begin the task of converting the Mexican Indians to Christianity.

To the Spanish, like many Europeans at the end of the Middle Ages, separation of church and state was an unknown concept. After more than seven hundred years of domination by the infidel Moors, the Reconquest of Spain was completed under Ferdinand and Isabella in 1492. Many Spaniards saw the discovery of the New World as a religious reward for their centuries of struggle.

Some Spanish clergy advocated the extinction of all vestiges of native traditions because they were heathen; others were more tolerant and even adapted aspects of native religions to Christianity. In ancient Mexico, a long tradition of adopting the deities of conquering and conquered tribes had existed, creating an extensive pantheon by the time of the Spanish Conquest. Attributes of some pre-Hispanic gods were integrated with those of Christian saints introduced by the Spanish missionaries. As early as 1519, on the Mexican island of Cozumel off the coast of Yucatán, Cortés replaced the image of the Mayan moon goddess in the local temple with a statue of the Virgin of the Immaculate Conception.[1] A crescent moon is one of the main attributes of this representation of the Virgin Mary. The correspondence must have been apparent to Spaniards and Indians alike.

The religious philosophy of the Indians of central Mexico included significant concepts similar to Christian tenets.[2] They believed in an eternal life in which the soul continued to live in an afterworld. To them, however, heaven was not a reward, nor hell a punishment. The circumstances of one's death, rather than behavior during life, determined the nature of afterlife. Death in battle or childbirth were two of the more honorable ways to enter afterlife. The Aztecs also believed that their great god, Huitzilopochtli, was born of a virgin goddess. They held a vague belief in a supreme god or God of Gods, Ometeuctli. The cross was also a sacred sign. It symbolized the cardinal points of direction and served as an identifying attribute for the gods of wind and rain. The Mexican Indians also practiced rites similar to confession, baptism, and communion, and a celibate priesthood was dedicated to the administration of the religious needs of the public. Outward symbols of the native religions included temples with altars and three-dimensional representations of the various gods. Religious processions that included images of pagan deities were a common practice as well.

In December of 1531, ten years after the Spanish conquest of Mexico, a Christianized Indian named Juan Diego was walking to a Franciscan mission near Mexico City to receive instruction and hear Mass. As he climbed the hill at Tepeyac, formerly the site of a temple to the Aztec earth goddess, he heard birds singing and a lovely voice calling him by name. He followed the voice and came upon a young dark-skinned woman. According to Nahuatl folk legend recorded in the seventeenth century,

1. Victor Turner and Edith Turner, *Image and Pilgrimage in Christian Culture* (New York: Columbia University Press, 1978), pp. 50–51.
2. Robert Ricard, *The Spiritual Conquest of Mexico* (Berkeley: University of California Press, 1966), pp. 31–32.

Her garments were as brilliant as the sun;
the rock on which she stood was shot through
   with rays of the sun
and seemed like an anklet of precious stones,
and it reflected on the ground like a rainbow.
The mesquite trees, prickly pear, and the
   other plants that grow there,
seemed to be made of emeralds;
their leaves of fine turquoises;
and their branches and thorns were
   as brilliant as gold.
He knelt before her and heard her soft
   and courteous voice
which charmed and awed him very much.[3]

She told him that she was the Mother of the True God and that she wanted a temple to be built on the hill of Tepeyac from which she could aid Juan Diego and his fellow countrymen. She bade him go to the bishop of Mexico, Fray Juan de Zumárraga, and give him her message. Zumárraga received Juan Diego and listened attentively to his story but told him to come back another time. Juan Diego returned to the hill of Tepeyac and begged the Virgin to send a more influential and worthy representative to the bishop. She replied that he was her choice and bade him visit the bishop again. This time Zumárraga asked Juan Diego to bring proof of his encounter with the Virgin.

When Juan Diego relayed the message to the Virgin on December 12, she told him to climb to the top of the hill, pick the flowers there, and take them to the bishop. Since it was winter, Juan Diego was astonished to find the hilltop covered with Castillian roses in full bloom. He filled his *tilma*, a maguey-fiber cloak, and took the roses to Bishop Zumárraga. When Juan Diego opened his tilma to release the roses, an image of the beautiful dark-skinned Virgin miraculously appeared on the fabric. The bishop had the image enshrined in his chapel until a church could be constructed on the hill of Tepeyac, as the Virgin had requested. She became known as the Virgin of Guadalupe (Frontispiece).

The fact that the young Virgin appeared to an Indian and was dark-skinned herself naturally made her popular among the Indians. A quotation from the English sailor, Miles Philips, shows that both Spaniards and Indians alike were devoted to the Virgin of Guadalupe from soon after her appearance. Abandoned by Sir John Hawkins on the Gulf coast of Mexico in 1568, Philips and his companions were captured by the Spanish and taken to Mexico City. In his diary, Philips described the reverence for the Virgin of Guadalupe that he witnessed.

---

3. Bernardo Bergoend, S.J., *La Nacionalidad Mexicana y la Virgen de Guadalupe*, 2nd ed. (México: Editorial Jus, 1968), p. 47. Translation from Spanish is by this author.

Whensoever any Spaniards pass by this church, although they be on horseback, they will alight, and come into the church, and kneel before this image, and pray to our Lady to defend them from all evil; so whether he be horseman or footman he will not pass by, but first go into the church and pray as aforesaid, which if they do not, they think and believe that they shall never prosper: which image they call in the Spanish tongue, Nuestra Señora de Guadalupe.[4]

The Virgin of Guadalupe has been credited with numerous miracles over the centuries, including the curing of a wounded Indian as early as 1531 and delivering Mexico City from a disastrous flood in 1621 and a plague in 1737. Pilgrimages to the miraculous image of the Virgin of Guadalupe began shortly after her appearance (Figs. 3, 11).

Pilgrimage was an ancient tradition in Mexico. Several modern Christian sites in Mexico had been pilgrimage centers before the conquest as well. In the sixteenth century, Bishop Diego de Landa of Yucatán compared the indigenous pilgrimages to Chichén Itzá and Cozumel with the Christian pilgrimages to Rome and Jerusalem.[5] The similarity to European traditions was not lost on the early missionaries, and native pilgrimage traditions were sometimes assimilated to aid the conversion to Catholicism. Today pilgrims from different regions of Mexico travel together at specific times each year to visit particular shrines in a form of group pilgrimage that was customary before the conquest. The annual dates seem to be related to events in the Aztec ritual calendar.

Christ figures are venerated at some pilgrimage centers such as Christ on the Cross at Chalma, Christ in the Sepulchre at Sacromonte in Amecameca, and the Christ Child at Plateros, Zacatecas. Different representations of the Virgin Mary are also honored, and various saints are likewise revered as wonder-working images.

Many material expressions of devotion are hung in pilgrimage centers (Fig. 4). At Chalma and Sacromonte, for instance, it is customary for parents to offer umbilical cords of newborns contained in cloth bags. These mementos may derive from traditions associated with Cihuacoatl, the pre-Hispanic goddess of childbirth. Ex-votos—paintings on wood, canvas, or tin—commemorate miraculous interventions by specific cult images (Figs. 4, 10). *Milagros*—small votive offerings of tin, silver, or gold—are pledged in thanksgiving for special requests fulfilled (Figs. 16, 66). Personal mementos such as crutches, braces, casts, articles of clothing, charms, children's shoes, and championship sports trophies or uniforms are often donated in gratitude for divine assistance.

Many pilgrims wear wreaths of paper flowers during the last mile of their journey and drop to their knees during the final approach to a shrine (Figs. 11, 14). Groups from all parts of the country journey to pilgrimage sites to perform costumed dances that combine pre-Hispanic and Christian traditions. Special markets cater to the needs of

4. Richard Hakluyt, *Principal Navigations, Voyages, Traffiques, and Discoveries of the English Nation* (1589), ed. by Edmund Goldsmid (Edinburgh: Goldsmid, 1884–90), vol. XIV, p. 205.

5. J. Eric S. Thompson, *The Rise and Fall of Maya Civilization*, 2nd ed. (Norman: University of Oklahoma Press, 1966), p. 135.

visitors to pilgrimage centers (Figs. 7, 25).

Since the early colonial period, special Masses and processions have been organized in Mexico to avert disaster. In 1736–37 a devastating plague struck Mexico City. Local officials and clergy appealed for aid to the Virgin of Loretto, and then to the Virgin of Remedios (Succor). Finally, the image of the Virgin of Guadalupe was solemnly declared "Patroness of the City of Mexico" and transported in procession from Tepeyac to the Cathedral of Mexico. The plague miraculously ceased, and devotion to the Virgin of Guadalupe increased in the mid-eighteenth century. Between 1576 and 1922, the well-known image of the Virgin of Remedios (Succor) traveled from her church on the outskirts of Mexico City to the cathedral on the main plaza approximately seventy-five times in supplication for deliverance from various calamities.[6]

The early missionaries used religious theater as a teaching tool in the Christianization of the Indians. Extravagant productions in native languages, called *autos*, were staged throughout the year and for special occasions. Complex stage-sets were built and colorfully decorated while local Indians acted the character parts. In one production in the sixteenth century a cast of more than eight hundred enacted *The Last Judgement* in Mexico City. In Tlajomulco, near Guadalajara, an Indian man played the same part for over thirty years in the annual production of *The Adoration of the Kings* during the late sixteenth century.[7] Derived from medieval mystery and Passion plays and related to European romance literature, topics presented in these religious dramas included the Annunciation to the Virgin, the Fall of Adam and Eve, the Sacrifice of Isaac, the Capture of Jerusalem, and the Passion of Christ.

Probably inspired by elaborate stage sets for Christmas plays, large nativity scenes have been constructed in churches and courtyards since the sixteenth century (Fig. 35). Parishioners contribute objects to the village scene and landscape that surround the Holy Family in the manger. From early December through Epiphany miniature figures and animals to be placed in the nativity scenes are sold at local markets and by street vendors (Figs. 29–31). In many villages in Mexico, people still dress in costumes and play the parts of Mary and Joseph searching for room in an inn in *Las Posadas*, the shepherds in *Los Pastores*, or the three kings in *Los Tres Reyes Magos*.

Lenten and Holy Week traditions were introduced to Mexico from Europe where Spain itself retained many medieval traditions that had fallen into disuse in many other areas. In many villages and cities of Spain, most notably in Seville, elaborate processions are still conducted from Palm Sunday through Easter Sunday. On those days, wooden sculptures of figures from the Passion of Christ are dressed in special clothing and carried on platforms through the streets. Individual sculptures of the Virgin of Sorrows, with gilded haloes, embroidered capes, and even crystal tears, are carried on canopied floats covered with fresh flowers and candles. Intricate scenes involving life-size sculptures are

6. Turner and Turner, p. 70.

7. Motolinía (Fray Toribio de Benavente), *Motolinía's History of the Indians of New Spain*, trans. by Francis Borgia Steck (Washington, D.C.: Academy of American Franciscan History, 1951), pp. 154–67.

arranged on large gilded floats or *pasos*. Represented in this pageant are events from the Passion of Christ such as the Last Supper, the Arrest in the Garden of Gethsemane, Christ before Pilate, the Road to Calvary, the Crucifixion, the Entombment, and the Resurrection. Arrangements may include Roman soldiers mounted on life-size sculptures of horses.

The floats are paid for and organized by lay religious confraternities, or *cofradías*, associated with local churches. Members of the brotherhoods carry the floats or march in procession wearing robes with pointed hoods in the colors of the various cofradías, or dressed as Roman soldiers. Many carry candles, Instruments of the Passion, or large crosses as acts of penance. In earlier times flagellation was a common practice during Holy Week processions. In some villages in Spain, the medieval tradition of the Passion play survives, and townspeople dress in costume and reenact the events of the Passion in dramatic productions.

Holy Week processions in Mexico during the sixteenth century were described by the Augustinian friar, Juan de Grijalva:

The confraternities of penance, and the processions of Lent, are admired by all who see them. It seems a work of art to see the order and the silence in them with so many devotional images, so many tender pasos, so many candles, so many banners. . . . Each paso is like a live representation: with the Seizure in the Garden, the Crowning with Thorns, the Flagellation, the Nailing to the Cross—all carved sculptures of great value and devotion.[8]

Several towns in Mexico are still renowned for their extensive Holy Week celebrations and processions, such as Taxco, Ixtapalapa, and Tzintzuntzan.

In many towns, sculptures of Christ's Entry into Jerusalem are elaborately decorated and carried in procession on Palm Sunday (Figs. 55, 69). The churches and streets are strewn with palm leaves, and bystanders carry decorative ornaments made of palm leaves woven in intricate patterns (Fig. 58). Palm Sunday processions in Mexico were described in the sixteenth century by Fray Toribio de Benavente, called Motolinía.

On Palm Sunday they decorate all the churches with palms. . . . It is interesting to see the different devices into which they fashion their palms. Over the palm many place crosses made of flowers, and these appear in a thousand shapes and in many colors. Others have the palms themselves entwined with roses and flowers of various forms and colors. Since the palms are green and they carry them aloft in their hands, it looks like a forest. . . . Up the trees the boys climb, some cutting off branches and strewing them along the road when the crosses pass by; others, perched in the trees, are singing. . . .[9]

In all villages in Spain and Mexico, sculpted images in churches are specially dressed, often in the colors of Lent—purple, white, red, black—and decorated with

8. Fray Juan de Grijalva, *Crónica de la Orden de N. P. S. Augustin en las provincias de la Nueva España*, 1624 (México: Robledo, 1924). Translation by author.

9. Motolinía, p. 143.

streamers and flowers (Figs. 19, 57). Often blazing candles are placed before them. At other times during Lent, certain sculptures, and sometimes entire altars, are draped in purple or black and then unveiled for a specific Mass (Figs. 62, 64). Throughout the Lenten season, sculptures of relevant saints are frequently grouped together on special altars or in prominent locations in churches as if frozen in perpetual reenactment of the Passion (Figs. 53, 65, 71). Special altars called *Incendios* (Passion or Fire) are dedicated to the sorrows of the Virgin. They include containers of growing wheat grass, representing the Body of Christ which will become the Bread of the Eucharist, and small gold flags, symbolizing purity and that which is most precious to the Virgin Mary (Figs. 9, 52).

In many villages, small processions take place with only one or two Passion sculptures carried by townspeople. On occasion, villagers dress as characters of the Passion and continue the medieval tradition of reenacting the Passion play (Fig. 49).

On Saturday during Holy Week large papier-mache effigies of Judas the Traitor are wired with fireworks and ceremonially burned in several villages in Mexico (Fig. 59). Ritual burning of effigies occurred in medieval Europe, the Witch of Winter being the most common image. The tradition survives today in some villages in Italy, France, and Spain. Large papier-mâché figures known as *gigantes* or *cabezudos* play a part in Corpus Christi processions in Spain, most notably in Toledo, although they are not burned. Among the Aztecs in pre-Hispanic Mexico, effigies of gods were constructed of a paste made of amaranth seed. These were paraded through towns and then ceremonially eaten by the devout. This practice was strictly forbidden in sixteenth-century Mexico, but the concept of making effigies has survived in the form of the Judas figure.

Throughout the calendar year, other religious celebrations are held in communities across Mexico. The feast day of the patron saint of towns or churches is always a particularly festive occasion. Streets, churches, and saints are decorated for a special Mass and procession (Figs. 26, 45, 50). Church decorations in the sixteenth century were described by Motolinía who mentioned green boughs, flowers, reed mace, sedge, and described floors strewn with fresh mint (Fig. 51).[10]

Motolinía also described the street decorations for a Corpus Christi procession in the town of Tlaxcala in 1538.

The Most Holy Sacrament was carried in procession together with many crosses and litters bearing the images of Saints. The drapes on the crosses and the trimmings on the litters were of gold and feather-work. The statues on the litters had the same adornments which in Spain, on account of their fine workmanship, would have been more highly prized than brocade. There were many banners of the Saints. . . . Many of those who took part in the procession carried lighted candles. The entire road was covered with sedge and mace reeds and flowers, while someone kept strewing roses and carnations, and many kinds of dances enlivened the procession. On the road there were chapels with their altars and retables, well

10. Motolinía, p. 141.

*adorned, where pauses were made during the procession. A boys' choir sang and danced
before the Most Holy Sacrament.*[11]

Religious processions and ritual dances are still performed during feast day celebrations
(Figs. 46–48). Following the folk saying "misa y mesa" (Mass and table), the solemn
activities are followed by lively festivals which include carnivals, feasting, music, and
social dances. Evident in these celebrations is the merger of both European and local
Mexican traditions creating the rich and unique quality of Mexican Catholicism.

In all cultures, sacred allegories and myths are expressed through ritual. Age-old
Christian narratives are retold each year. In Mexico the retelling is not merely verbal but
also visual and participatory. Parishioners or images of saints dramatize the stories of the
Bible. Sculptures grouped together in churches remind people of the seasonal story to be
contemplated. Processions, whether somber or celebratory, bring the religious narrative
out of the church and into the streets. Music and ritual dances either celebrate miracles or
express sorrow and penance. In religious dramas, townspeople reenact the events of the
Old and New Testament as well as the lives of the saints. The communal reliving of
the Christian story is mirrored in the ever-changing decorations of the churches and
saints. Throughout the year worshippers in Mexico constantly witness and participate in
this living ritual.

11. Motolinía, p. 152.

Mexican Celebrations

1. Ruins of former Dominican mission church, Cuilapan, Oaxaca.

2. Virgin of Guadalupe in cemetery,
Ocotlán, Tlaxcala.

3. Kneeling women, former Basilica of
Guadalupe, Mexico City.

4. Ex-voto paintings and other mementos offered in thanksgiving for petitions granted by the Christ of Villaseca, in the pilgrimage church at the entrance to the famous silver mine, La Cata, Guanajuato.

5. Haystack with recessed cross, near
Tlaxcala, Tlaxcala.

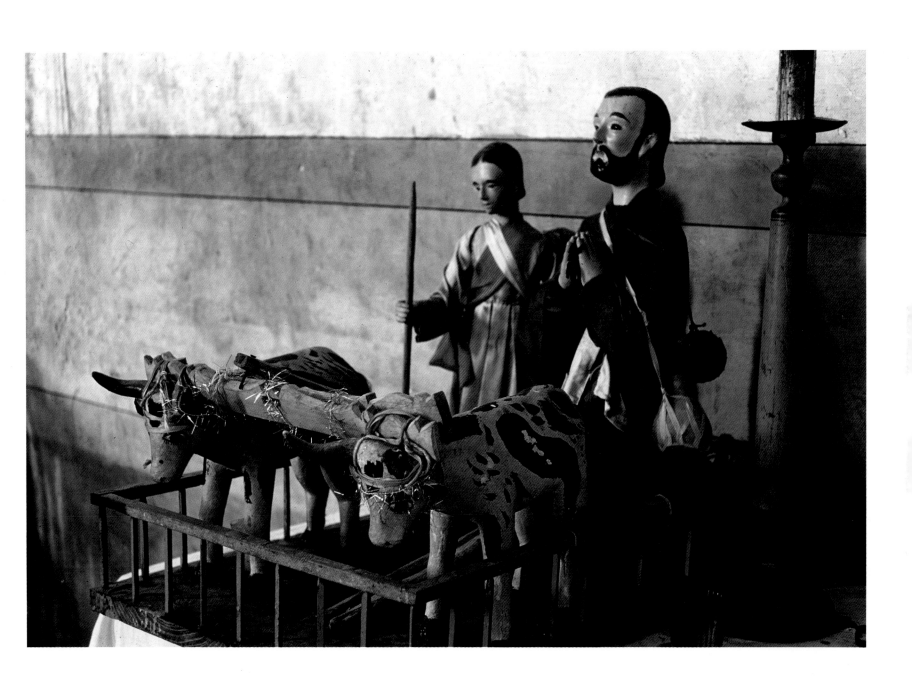

6. Saint Isidore, patron saint of farmers,
with his oxen and the angel who plowed
his fields while he prayed, parish church,
Naranja de Tapia, Michoacán.

7. Religious images for sale, San Juan de
los Lagos, Jalisco.

8. Paper flower wreaths placed in cemetery on Day of the Dead or All Soul's Day on November 2, cemetery near Jalapa, Veracruz.

9. Main altar, church of Santa María Tonanzintla, Puebla. The square gold flags symbolize that which is most precious (Christ) and are part of the *Incendios* (Passion or Fire) altars to the Sorrows of the Virgin erected during Lent.

10. Ex-voto paintings crediting the Virgin of Guadalupe for divine assistance with train accidents, the police, bandits, fires, and modern surgery, Basilica of Guadalupe, Mexico City.

Ex-voto painting documenting assistance from the Virgin of Guadalupe when a ship was threatened by a storm off the west coast of Mexico in March 1913, Basilica of Guadalupe, Mexico City.

11. Pilgrims advancing on their knees to the former Basilica of Guadalupe built at the end of the seventeenth century. A new basilica to house the miraculous image of the Virgin of Guadalupe was constructed close by in the 1980s.

12. Draped pulpit in former Augustinian mission church of Saint Augustine, Acolman, Mexico.

13. Easter Mass in the former Augustinian mission church of Saint Augustine, Acolman, Mexico.

14. Feather duster, cleaning pail, and wreath of artificial flowers, entrance to pilgrimage church, Atotonilco, Guanajuato. Wreaths are worn by the faithful for special occasions such as pilgrimages, weddings, first communions, and feast days.

15. Man kneeling before an image of the Virgin of Remedios (Succor), parish church of San Miguel in a village near Jalapa, Veracruz.

16. Altar of Saint Lucy, church of La Salud (Health), San Miguel de Allende, Guanajuato. St. Lucy was blinded during martyrdom, so she is invoked to cure eye ailments. Small votive offerings of eyes (milagros) have been placed along the edge of the picture frame.

17. Our Lady of the Sacred Heart, church of Cuilapan, Oaxaca. The Sacred Heart of Mary is a rather late devotional image that became popular in the eighteenth and nineteenth centuries. Like most images, its cult was spread through devotional prints such as the one seen on the altar here.

18. Christ in Distress (Paciencia) with processional banner and lanterns during Lent, parish church of San Jerónimo, Tlacochahuaya, Oaxaca. This passion image represents Christ seated at Calvary while the cross is being assembled for His crucifixion.

19. Saint Anthony and the Christ Child, parish church of Santa Helena de Xoxocotlán, Oaxaca. The Christ Child is clothed in a purple and white dress for Lent, and a Lenten banner has been left on the altar. Beneath them is a painting of the Holy Trinity as three identical men. Such representations of the Trinity were banned by papal decree in 1745, but can still be seen in Mexico today.

20. Christ Child Enthroned, in a church near the plaza, Oaxaca, Oaxaca. Worshippers have placed toy animals and marbles on the altar for the Holy Child.

21. Virgin and Child, the Youthful
Saint John the Baptist, and probably
Saint Vincent of Zaragoza, Deacon,
church of Ixtepec, Oaxaca.

22. Virgin of the Immaculate Conception, flanked by flower wreaths, Templo de Jesús, Naranja de Tapia, Michoacán.

23. Church and market, Izúcar de
Matamoros, Puebla.

24. Fruit juice and food vendor, Feast of the Virgin of Guadalupe, December 12, Guadalajara, Jalisco.

25. Photographer's horse, equipment,
and backdrop with painting of the image
and pilgrimage church of Our Lady of
Saint John of the Lakes, San Juan de los
Lagos, Jalisco.

26. Christmas decorations, Yuririapúndaro, Guanajuato. Streets in Mexico often remain decorated throughout the Christmas season, from the Feast of the Virgin of Guadalupe on December 12 through Epiphany or the Feast of the Three Kings on January 6.

27. Flower and vegetable vendor in the market, Oaxaca, Oaxaca. During Lent churches and saints are often decorated with purple and white flowers.

28. Paper doves for sale during Christmas season, Querétaro, Querétaro.

29. Plant vendor during Christmas season, Querétaro, Querétaro. Moss, cacti, and other greenery are used for landscape in nativity scenes.

30. Toys and masks for sale in the market during Christmas season, Querétaro, Querétaro.

31. Nativity scene figurines for sale during Christmas season, Guadalajara, Jalisco.

32. Boy selling streamers during Christmas season, Querétaro, Querétaro.

33. Fireworks in front of the church of San Francisco de Asís on Christmas night, Querétaro, Querétaro.

34. Christmas decorations at the entrance to the Church of San Francisco, Mexico City.

35. Nativity scene set up in a church
Querétaro, Querétaro.

36. Toys for sale in market during Christmas season, Morelia, Michoacán. As in Spain, children in Mexico often receive toys on January 6, the Feast of the Three Kings, rather than on Christmas Day.

37. Papier-mâché horses on wheels for
sale in market during Christmas season,
Morelia, Michoacán.

38. Ribbon stand in market, Mérida, Yucatán.

39. Christmas decorations, church of La Salud, San Miguel de Allende, Guanajuato.

40. Lenten decorations, side aisle, former Dominican mission church of Santo Domingo, Chiapa de Corzo, Chiapas.

41. Palm Sunday decorations, church of
San Felipe, Mexico.

42. Virgin with Lenten decorations, Templo de Jesús, Naranja de Tapia, Michoacán.

43. Cloth streamers before main altar with image of Saint James, Conqueror of the Moors, Chapel of Santiago, Amozoc, Puebla. Although Saint James is usually represented astride a white horse, the horse is missing here.

44. Lenten decorations, Templo de
Jesús, Naranja de Tapia, Michoacán.

45. Street decorations for the Feast of
the Virgin of Guadalupe, December 12,
Guadalajara, Jalisco.

46. Spectators view the celebration in
honor of the Day of the Virgin of Guadalupe from every available vantage point.
Impersonating a female character is a
man dressed in pink, December 11, 1955,
Tepic, Nayarit.

47. Clown and spectators in front of
church gate. Twisted garlands of pine
needles adorn the entrance for Guadalupe Day and the coming Christmas
season, Tepic, Nayarit.

48. Dancers wearing crowns and elegant dress parade through the street carrying banners. Some of the faithful walk on their knees as penance to honor the Virgin, Guadalupe Day festival, Tepic, Nayarit.

49. Masked dancers pause during their performance of a Judas pageant on Holy Saturday during Holy Week. March 31, 1956, Atotonilco el Grande, Hidalgo.

50. Street decorations for the Feast of the
Virgin of Guadalupe, December 12,
Guadalajara, Jalisco.

51. Interior of church, Amatenango del Valle, Chiapas. The floor is covered with greenery for Ash Wednesday services on the first day of Lent.

52. The Virgin of Sorrows and Mary Magdalen, dressed and placed at the foot of the cross during Lent, church of Santa María Tonanzintla, Puebla. A traditional *Incendio* (Passion or Fire) altar to the Sorrows of the Virgin has been set up with gold flags symbolizing purity and preciousness, flowers, and potted wheat plants representing the bread of the Eucharist.

53. Crucifixion, church in San Miguel de Allende, Guanajuato. Christ is flanked by the two thieves; the Virgin Mary, Saint John the Evangelist, and Mary Magdalen appear at the foot of the cross. The oil painting on the wall behind the sculptures depicts the city of Jerusalem with the eclipse of the sun above.

54. Christ of the Passion in a glass niche, in a church in San Miguel de Allende, Guanajuato. Many Passion figures, particularly of Christ, have articulated arms and legs and can be placed in various positions for the reenactment of the Stations of the Cross.

55. Christ's Entry into Jerusalem riding
an ass, church of Ixtepec, Oaxaca.

56. Mary Magdalen, dressed in purple and white for Lent, parish church of San Jerónimo, Tlacochahuaya, Oaxaca. The Magdalen frequently has long red hair donated by a worshipper as a votive offering. Although not visible in the photograph, this image of the Magdalen was paired with a statue of the Virgin of Sorrows dressed in black.

57. Lenten decorations in church of
Santa María de Coyotepec, Oaxaca.

58. Vendors selling woven palm decorations for Palm Sunday in front of the Cathedral of Mexico, Mexico City.

59. Judas effigy wired with fireworks for burning during Holy Week, near Atotonilco el Grande, Hidalgo.

60. Lamb of God placed on roof of church during Lent, El Tule, Oaxaca.

61. Christ on the Cross, cloister of former Augustinian mission church of San Nicolás, Actopan, Hidalgo.

62. Main altár screen shrouded in purple for Holy Week, former Franciscan mission church of San Bernardino, Xochimilco, Mexico.

63. The Mourning Virgin, former Augustinian mission church of Saint Augustine, Acolman, Mexico.

64. Christ on the Cross and other images draped in purple for Lent, parish church of San Antonio, Córdoba, Veracruz.

65. Passion figures on litters for Holy Week processions, parish church of San Miguel Xochitl, Mexico.

66. Christ in the Sepulchre with metal
votive offerings (milagros), Dominican
church of Santo Domingo, Puebla,
Puebla.

67. Images shrouded for Lent, former Dominican mission church of Santo Domingo, Yanhuitlán, Oaxaca.

68. Sixteenth-century painting of Holy Week processions on the nave wall, former Franciscan mission church of San Miguel, Huejotzingo, Puebla. The penitents wear the hooded robes of different confraternities. The marchers in black carry the Instruments of the Passion; the ones in white are flagellants and children.

69. Christ's Entry into Jerusalem riding an ass, decorated with paper flowers and palm leaves for Lent, Teotitlán del Valle, Oaxaca.

70. Christ of the Passion on an altar
screen, former Franciscan mission church
of San Miguel, Huejotzingo, Puebla.

71. Christ figures, Saint Francis, and the
Virgin of Sorrows, dressed for Lent in
purple and black, side altar, former
Franciscan mission church of San Miguel,
Huejotzingo, Puebla.

72. Christ carrying the Cross on the Road to Calvary, on a processional litter for Lent, Templo de Jesús, Naranja de Tapia, Michoacán.

73. Christ on the Cross, placed in a
prominent location for Lent in a village
church near Naranja de Tapia,
Michoacán.

74. Christ on the Cross, draped with white cloth for the Deposition from the Cross, during Lent, Teotitlán del Valle, Oaxaca.

75. Christ on the Cross before red drape, in cloister of the former Franciscan mission church of the Immaculate Conception, Izamal, Yucatán.

76. The Resurrected Christ, traditionally called Christ in Limbo when standing with a banner, church of Hoctún, Yucatán.

77. During Carnival, at the beginning of Lent, festival captains dance around their town to the tune of the flute. They carry red banners and shaved wooden staffs as the signs of their office. February 12, 1956, Tenejapa, Chiapas.

78. Indian women carrying their children on their backs during Carnival. The women wear their traditional handwoven decorated blouses and wrap skirts. Tenejapa, Chiapas.

79. At the Carnival festival, the dancing flag bearers are identified by their red suits and red banners. Tenejapa, Chiapas.

80. Carnival celebrants in front of the
church, Tenejapa, Chiapas.

81. Church and people of Chamula, a Tzotzil-speaking Maya community in the highlands of Chiapas.

82. People gather in the plaza for the
Carnival events and accompanying market. Chamula men wear the traditional
dress of white short trousers and shirt,
handwoven sleeveless overshirt, sandals,
and the hat of the region.

83. Chamula Indian woman in traditional dress. Women are usually the spectators during ceremonial events. Carnival at Chamula, Chiapas.

84. Chamula man and woman. Traditional thatched roof houses surround the area beyond the plaza. Chamula, Chiapas.

85. Festival participants called Monkeys and unattached Free Monkeys roam the plaza during Carnival at Chamula, Chiapas.

86. During Carnival in Chamula Christ and the Virgin are represented by sacred silver lance tips with flag "clothing." Chamula, Chiapas.

87. The red-suited lance bearer, called a
Passion, is an important religious officer
who is completing his yearly term. He is
accompanied by his assistants, called
Monkeys, who wear hats made of monkey
fur. Carnival at Chamula, Chiapas.

88. Crowds of onlookers flock around the
religious officers and the sacred lances
during Carnival. Chamula, Chiapas.

89. On the last day before Lent (Shrove Tuesday) the cargueros and their assistants run through a fire of burning thatch in the plaza as a rite of purification. If a runner falls into the fire, it is punishment from the deities for wrongdoing during the year. Carnival, Chamula, Chiapas.

90. Participants visit one of several cross shrines, probably representing the Stations of the Cross, during Carnival in Chamula, Chiapas.

The Making of a Festival

"I am a farmer. But once a year I become something else." This statement was made by a dancer as he dressed himself to participate in the masked festival of the patron saint of his village of Juxtlahuaca, Oaxaca.[1] By this expression he reveals the basis of the festival concept. Festival must be different from everyday, a time when daily routine is set aside. People behave in ways dissimilar from their norm. They dress in their finest clothing, sometimes replacing Westernized clothing with their traditional regional costume; they elaborate and change their spaces at home, in the church or chapel, beautifying them by decorating with flowers, streamers, candles, and burning incense. Special objects are made or unpacked and freshened. Thoughts and feelings are intensified, all of the senses are stimulated, and awareness is heightened, as the community focuses on the celebration.

Celebration is a part of being human. All known cultures of the world celebrate, and Mexico is certainly no exception. Festival is integral to the Mexican life-style, with hundreds of fiestas taking place each year. The calendar year is organized according to festivals, and people purchase calendar books to keep track of the special days. They occur on the occasion of important religious holidays and patron saints' feasts, as well as patriotic anniversaries and civic events, although religious occasions outweigh secular ones in this very religious country. Individual communities emphasize certain feasts over others; however, Christmas, Lent and Holy Week, and All Saints' and All Souls' (popularly referred to as the Day of the Dead) are times of major celebrations throughout the country.

Festivals involve the entire community. The successful outcome of the celebration depends upon the effort of many people and careful planning, sometimes beginning a year in advance. Responsibility for supervising and financing the festival is assumed by sponsors or hosts, who serve with the approval of the community. The individual ritual term of office is called a *cargo*, meaning burden, and the officer a *carguero* or, in other locales, a *mayordomo, fiestero, encarguero, capitán,* or *comisionado* (Fig. 87).

A religious officer is usually a male member of the community who must be married before he can participate. His wife serves with him. In addition to hosting the festival the couple is concerned with the care and clothing of the community saints, and the maintenance of the church or chapel throughout the year. Ritual officers often complete their term of office at festival time when the new officers assume their obligations. An individual may serve several terms of office during a lifetime, and, if he advances through

1. James M. Burns and Betty Ann Brown, "Fiesta! A Mixtec Indian Festival in Mexico," videotape, 1980.

various levels of the ritual hierarchy, may ultimately become an elder with great influence in his community.

No one person or couple is able to assume sole responsibility for the festival. The host and his spouse must rely on the help of the entire family, as well as friends and those with whom they have a special relationship. All of these people can be counted on to provide kitchen space, contributions of ingredients, cooking utensils, firewood, time and expertise, refreshments and entertainment for the workers and participants. Cooperation among groups of people working together to prepare and execute a successful festival is one of the most important results of the celebration. Groups working together achieve community renewal and group pride and satisfaction.

Members of the community are responsible for various aspects of the festival depending on their expertise. Musicians and dance groups rehearse while costumes are sewn. Mothers, sisters, wives, or girlfriends make new costumes or repair and freshen last year's. Sometimes an order is placed with a specialist who makes costumes for others in the community. If the festival includes a masked dance, the male participants may carve or repaint their own masks, borrow or rent masks from someone else, or order a new mask from a local maskmaker. Most maskmakers in Mexico have other jobs and only make masks on a part-time basis, often during the off-season of the agricultural cycle. Both the wearers of the masks and the carvers are generally males. It is unusual to see a woman wearing a mask in a dance. Even when the impersonator represents a female, it is likely to be a male playing the part (Fig. 46).

Other arts in addition to masks and costumes are essential ingredients that identify the festival occasion. Fireworks provide not only visual excitement but also sound. The explosion is used to announce important moments during the festival. Mexico is renowned for its fireworks, in particular, the tall *castillo* (castle), sometimes reaching a height of fifty feet, which ends many festivals with wheels whirling and shooting fountains of sparks flying in all directions. Small boys wearing lighted armatures of fireworks in the shape of bulls race into the crowd, scattering the spectators.

Everywhere candles and incense in burners stimulate the sense of smell. Candles of all sizes, ranging from votives in glasses painted with images of saints to wax pillars as large as fence posts, are on sale in the open-air markets and shops. Many, made especially for the occasion, are decorated with colored foil paper and ribbons. *Copal*, a type of tree resin, is the most common incense. Its distinctive odor is a familiar festival aroma all over Mexico.

The weekly and daily local markets swell with festival-specific goods in the weeks before. Everything necessary for the special occasion is available. Hand-made folk arts such as figures made from palm leaves for Holy Week, pottery figures for Christmas Nativity scenes, sugar and pumpkin paste candies and toys for the Day of the Dead, and cut-out paper streamers make their appearance. The vendors are often sold out by the time the festival begins.

Ephemeral, or impermanent, arts are created specifically for festival occasions. The creations are not intended to last beyond the lifetime of the occasion, even though they may involve large quantities of labor and expense. Pathways and archways, where the procession bearing the saints will pass, are constructed of vegetal and perishable materials. Flower petal and colored sawdust carpets last only as long as it takes for the procession to pass by. Archways are covered with oranges and other fruits, flowers, and leaves. Strewn on the floors of churches, pine needles give off a pleasant aroma as the worshipper walks upon them while twisted pine needle garlands hang overhead (Fig. 51). Pathways of marigold petals lead directly from the street through the front door of the home to the altar inside to assist the dead soul in finding its way on the Day of the Dead.

Cut flowers are even more abundant than usual at festival time. The images of the saints, Jesus, and the Virgin Mary receive quantities of floral bouquet offerings on church altars and home altars. On some occasions such as the Day of the Dead, particularly elaborate home altars are constructed as an important focus for the season's devotion. Elaborately shaped and decorated breads and candies are another type of ephemeral art which accompanies celebrations in Mexico.

Feasting is a recurrent element of festival throughout the world. In Mexico large quantities of food are prepared to feed performers, family, and guests. The display of generosity and hospitality, abundance and prosperity is important to the success of the festival. In the villages women and girls prepare the food in outdoor kitchens, cooking in enormous clay pots, which they stir with long-handled wooden spoons, directly over open wood fires.

Lavish festival meals differ from those of everyday. Special and luxury foods are served, such as meat, chocolate, sweet white flour breads in special shapes, and fruits from other regions. Red flags hang over the doorways of community butcher shops announcing that fresh meat is available. *Mole*, a pre-Hispanic dish of chicken in a thick red chile and chocolate sauce, is served throughout Mexico. Ritual drinking is another unifying activity of the festival. Bottled sodas, beer, and distilled liquors are plentiful.

Religious festivals are expensive. At a festival which I witnessed in 1987, the mayordomo informed me that the festival cost $1,000. This is a tremendous expense in a country where the annual average income was $525 before the devaluation of the peso in the early 1980s.[2] For the festival sponsor the expenditure represents a substantial part of their earnings. Although the sponsor may be assisted by donations from family and community members who are honored by dancers performing in front of their house, nevertheless the sponsor and his family must be prepared to fund a major portion of the celebration. In this way the wealth of the community is periodically redistributed among its members, and the wealthier share their good fortune with the community in homage and thanksgiving to the saints.

2. Priscilla Rachun Linn, "Chamula Carnival: The 'Soul' of Celebration," in *Celebration: Studies in Festivity and Ritual*, edited by Victor Turner (Washington, D.C.: Smithsonian Institution Press, 1982), pp. 191–92.

A couple may volunteer to sponsor the next year's festival in response to a promise, or vow, which they made to Christ, the Virgin Mary, or a saint, in return for a favor granted. Such favors include recuperation from an illness or an accident experienced personally, by a family member, or a farm animal; protection from a disaster; an abundant harvest, and continued good health. Sponsorship of a festival is also a means to accumulate good works to ensure entrance into heaven. Promises may also motivate young men to perform in arduous festival dances, pilgrims to travel long distances to a site of their devotion, and devotees to purchase or commission a *milagro* (metal votive offering) or ex-voto painting to be presented to the saint invoked.

A well-organized, ample, and beautiful festival is a source of pride to the community and is discussed and evaluated by its members. If the community judges the festival to be well presented, this reflects favorably on its sponsors and increases their standing and prestige in the community, thus allowing for an enlarged role in the leadership.

On the first day of the festival there is much activity in the community as final preparations are completed. Celebrations occur on specific cyclical occasions which are important to the community. Some festivals last only one day, but more often they occur over several days. Festivities often continue for an octave, which spans from the feast day to the following eighth day. During a major ritual season such as Lent or Christmas, activities may take place over a period of weeks.

Certain elements are common to most festivals in Mexico, notwithstanding the tremendous variety and diversity that exists within this formula. Performances such as masked or unmasked dances, dramas, and processions are anticipated elements of a Mexican festival. These events take place in public spaces. Usually the churchyard, the church interior, and the streets are the stage, and often the performers move through all of these spaces (Figs. 46–49).

The procession of community members and elders carrying the sacred images of the Virgin, Christ, and the saints winds slowly from the church or chapel through the streets, finally returning the images to their home. As the sacred objects are processed around and through the significant points of the community or barrio, purification and benediction are bestowed, renewing the defenses of the community against potential danger and evil. The young women, who often carry the litters of the images, are dressed in their finest, and bright and colorful decorations, perhaps fresh flowers, Christmas tinsel, or electric lights, adorn the saints' litters. The images, which are weighted down by several layers of fine clothing and jewelry, are sometimes barely visible. A brass band of musicians announces the presence of the entourage.

Dances, masked or unmasked, or dramas are usually a part of the celebration. In hundreds of Mexican communities masked dances have a prominent role in the festivals. The themes range from historic dramas, such as the conquering of Mexico by the Spanish, to the biblical reenactment of the Passion of Christ during Holy Week to animal and hunting dramas which include pre-Hispanic elements such as the jaguar warrior.

The two faces of the festival, solemn and festive, devout and playful, are often reflected in the dance itself. For example, stately, elegant dancers contrast with the humorous, outrageous clowns. This same dual element of contrast can be seen in the glittering ferris wheel and carnival, which often operate in the plaza immediately in front of the church.

The clowns, identifiable by their abnormal dress and their contrary behavior, are not simply entertainment nor a minor addition to the proceedings (Fig. 47). Rather they play an essential role in the proceedings, a role which is found throughout indigenous America and elsewhere as well. While appearing to be funny and licentious, they actually serve the serious purpose of protecting the customs and social order by turning, or inverting, the normal social order upside down. For example, male clowns dressed as females draw attention to appropriate feminine behavior by behaving in just the opposite manner. In other instances the clowns personify disorder, chaos, and potential evil which invade the community and ultimately are overcome by the close of the festival.

In general, young men are the performers, while the audience of women, children, and older men looks on. In many communities participation by young men in the festival dances and dramas marks their social transition from childhood to adulthood. Continuity of the tradition is ensured by younger boys who eagerly watch awaiting their turn to participate. Sometimes they have an opportunity to practice for a few hours, dressed in diminutive costumes.

Among the Tzotzil-speaking Maya Indians of San Juan Chamula in the Chiapas highlands, the five-day celebration of pre-Lenten Carnival is the most significant annual community celebration. Unlike the merrymaking and riotous behavior associated with Carnival celebrations elsewhere, the Chamula festival dramatizes the serious subjects of the life of Christ and the military history of the region. Office-holders, who sponsor the costly event, carry sacred flags and lances whose silver tips represent Christ, the Virgin Mary, and other sacred personages (Fig. 86). Cargueros and their assistants dress in costumes which recall historic soldiers' uniforms and Spanish gentlemen's attire (Fig. 87).

A complex series of militaristic dramas and dance events occurs throughout the "Festival of the Games," as it is termed by the Chamulas, while a barrage of fireworks, drums, and trumpets fills the air with noise. On the last day (Shrove Tuesday) the cargueros and their helpers and assistants run through a fire of burning thatch in the plaza as a rite of purification (Fig. 89). If a runner falls into the fire, it is in punishment by the deities for wrongdoing during the year.

Students of the Chamula Carnival remark that the festival presents Chamula's struggle to maintain cultural independence and identity.[3] This is one of the ongoing drives that causes Mexican festivals to continue to be an important part of Mexican folk life, as illustrated by the large numbers celebrated today. Clearly, they continue to serve the needs of the communities.

3. Ibid., p. 197.

Festivals are those special occasions, separated from everyday life, when members of the community refresh and reaffirm the significance and satisfaction of their lives. It is a time when performers and spectators share in a common experience. It is one way in which the group maintains its identity, distinct from that of other groups. Children are taught group values and social behavior. The participation of young people in some of the ritual activities marks their transition from childhood to adulthood. Groups work together, and in so doing reestablish old ties and form new ones. Individual social positions in the community are clarified. Participants repay their obligations to the saints through acts of service for restored health or good fortune during the year.

Eliot Porter and Ellen Auerbach visited and photographed Mexico in the 1950s. Thirty-five years later Eliot Porter asked me if I thought that the festivals of Mexico had changed since that time. My response must be yes, they have changed, just as all things must change over time and according to a variety of influences if they are to survive, but that does not imply that they have diminished. New materials such as polyester fabrics, plastics, rubber masks, booming radios, and loud speakers, to mention only a few examples, have been integrated into the occasions. While these introductions may give a more modern appearance to the celebration, and many mourn this incursion, maintaining that this spells doom or at the very least degeneration, to the participants themselves who will decide the fate of their festival, all is still "traditional" and therefore intact.

Beyond this, it becomes difficult to generalize since each community makes its own decisions regarding the importance of a strict adherence to custom. A change which may threaten the integrity of one community's festival may not be perceived as a danger in another community which is more open to introductions. From the time in 1956 when Porter and Auerbach photographed Carnival at Tenejapa, Chiapas (Fig. 77) to 1987 when a remarkably similar scene was photographed (Morris and Foxx 1987:191), great continuity in the costumes and the accoutrements of the dancers in Tenejapa is illustrated.[4] This suggests conservativism at Tenejapa when it comes to material change in rituals.

Historically, few observers recorded their impressions of Mexican festivals after the first great flush of reports which were sent back to Spain following the conquest. It remained until the late nineteenth century, when a few scientists began to investigate the various cultures of Mexico, for the living traditions to begin to be systematically recorded. From 1894 to 1904, Dr. Frederick Starr, an anthropologist at the University of Chicago, traveled to Mexico on a series of field trips. On occasion, Starr and his party stumbled upon villages that were in fiesta.

His fascination with the festivals of Mexico was clear. "The student of folk-lore can nowhere find a more interesting field for the study of popular celebration than our sister republic. We find there a most curious mingling of native American ideas and practices

4. Walter F. Morris and Jeffrey J. Foxx, *Living Maya* (New York: Harry N. Abrams, 1987).

with those of medieval Europe."[5] Starr's descriptions and photos provide nineteenth-century documentation for comparison with the same festivals today.

Celebrations in Mexico flourish today in small villages as well as in urban centers among the some fifty-seven different ethnic groups with their own languages and cultures. They are not mere retentions of the past, but rather active and essential ingredients in the lives of the Mexican people. The festivals mediate between the past and the future not only by giving its members a sense of tradition but also by providing continuity into the future. They are a source of pride and an important means for maintaining cultural and ethnic identity separate from the outside world and promoting social cohesion from within. They continue to be practiced because they are effective. Festival is serious business, albeit a very pleasurable one. Through festival the Mexican people celebrate themselves and their place in the universe.

5. Marsha C. Bol, "Mexican Masked Festivals at the Turn of the Century, as Witnessed by Frederick Starr," in *Behind the Mask in Mexico*, edited by Janet Brody Esser (Santa Fe: Museum of New Mexico Press, 1988), pp. 38–61.